The Power of Meekness

Mark Philps
Vicar of St Matthew's, Tipton

GROVE BOOKS LIMITED
RIDLEY HALL RD CAMBRIDGE CB3 9HU

Contents

1. Meekness and Power 3
2. The Biblical Basis of Meekness 7
3. The Meekness of Christ 10
4. The Power of Meekness 16
5. Growing in Meekness 22

Acknowledgements

My thanks to Charles Raven and Alison White of the Grove Spirituality Group for helpful comments on an earlier version of this booklet, and most of all to my wife, Caroline, for her constant encouragement to write it.

The Cover Illustration is by Peter Ashton

Copyright © Mark Philps 2000

First Impression May 2000
ISSN 0262-799X
ISBN 1 85174 432 0

1
Meekness and Power

Meekness has been out of favour for a long time. Most people believe that meekness is for losers and has nothing to teach a world where the big issue is power—its use and abuse. 'Meek' is an insult. A recent Easter advertising campaign in Britain portrayed Jesus as a Che Guevara figure with the caption 'Meek. Mild. As if.' Again, a report commissioned by the Archbishops of Canterbury and York on the nation's perception of the church characterized church spokesmen as 'meek and weak.'[1] The conjunction of those two words says it all: meekness, we have come to believe, is weakness. It denotes the feeble character who cannot or will not stand up to others. It suggests wimpishness at best and perhaps even downright cowardice.

The contention of this booklet is that this is a misunderstanding. Meekness is not primarily about how we relate to other people—it is a stance before God. It is supremely exemplified in the life of Jesus—a life of full-time obedience to and dependence upon God. It is a life of trust, in which God is acknowledged as both loving and sovereign, working out his purposes for us in all the circumstances which meet us. For that reason meekness is not weakness but a source of strength. Believing, with the apostle Paul, that 'all things work together for good for those who love God,' the meek person has the stability to face adversity and the strength to pursue the unpopular or uncomfortable option. And of course meekness does affect the way we treat other people. If we believe that our lives are watched over by a loving Father for whom nothing is too hard, then we do not always have to get our own way. The meek find much less need to push, shove and tread on their fellow human beings than others might—they are content to wait for God's time:

> The meek do not resent adversity because they accept everything as being the effect of God's wise and loving purpose for them, so that they accept injuries from men also…knowing that these are permitted by God for their ultimate good.[2]

Nietzsche

There are probably many reasons for the current misunderstanding of meekness—most of them outside the scope of this booklet. But I propose to touch on one of the most powerful influences involved—the German philosopher-poet Friedrich Nietzsche. Nietzsche hated the meekness preached by Christianity: 'These teachers of submission! Wherever there is anything small

---

[1] Quoted in *The Times*, 1 March 2000.
[2] *Illustrated Bible Dictionary*, Part 2: article 'Meekness' (Inter Varsity Press, 1980) p 972.

and sick and scabby, there they crawl like lice; and only my disgust stops me from cracking them.'[3] He has been profoundly influential in the 20th century—claimed as their own variously by 'anarchists, feminists, Nazis, religious cultists, Socialists, Marxists, vegetarians, avant-garde artists, devotees of physical culture, and archconservatives'[4] and now often described (with some justification) as the grandfather of postmodernism.

Nietzsche was brought up in a strict Lutheran family (his father was a pastor) but rebelled against Christianity. He later claimed 'I have absolutely no knowledge of atheism as an outcome of reasoning, still less as an event: with me it is obvious by instinct.'[5] His writing (mostly dating from the period 1872–1888) is elusive, teasing, self-contradictory, given to aphorism and exaggeration. So to some extent you can make Nietzsche mean what you want…

But there is a unifying theme running through Nietzsche's writing: his quest for what is life-giving and life-enhancing.[6] All other considerations were secondary—truth, morality, tradition, and values could and should be dispensed with if they proved anti-life. He believed that many if not all the traditional forms of authority in the culture of his day were no more than ways of controlling people—power games designed for the purpose of coercion: 'You exert power with your values and doctrines of good and evil, you assessors of values.'[7] God and religion in particular he saw as enemies of life and abuses of power:

> By saying 'God sees into the heart' [morality] denies the deepest and the highest desires of life and takes God for the *enemy of life*…Life is at an end where the 'kingdom of God' *begins*.[8]

The 'Will to Power' was for Nietzsche the fundamental dynamic of life. Even the renunciation of power, the desire to be a servant to others, is 'unmasked' by Nietzsche as just another kind of power game:

> Where I found a living creature, there I found will to power; and even in the will of the servant I found the will to be master.
>
> The will of the weaker persuades it to serve the stronger; its will wants to be master over those weaker still: this delight alone it is unwilling to forgo.
>
> And as the lesser surrenders to the greater, that it may have delight and power over the least of all, so the greatest, too, surrenders and for the sake of power stakes—life.

---

3   *Thus Spoke Zarathustra* (Penguin Classics, 1961) p 190.
4   Quoted in Michael Tanner, *Nietzsche* (OUP, 1994) p 1.
5   *Ecce Homo* (Penguin Books, 1992) p 21.
6   See Tanner, p 64.
7   *Thus Spoke Zarathustra*, p 139.
8   *Twilight of the Idols/The Antichrist* (Penguin Classics, 1990) p 55.

The devotion of the greatest is to encounter risk and danger and play dice for death.

And where sacrifice and service and loving glances are, there too is will to be master. There the weaker steals by secret paths into the castle and even into the heart of the more powerful—and steals power.[9]

It does not take much experience of human nature to agree with Nietzsche that service *can* be a form of manipulation—we will return to this theme when looking at codependency in chapter three. The problem is that Nietzsche appears to be saying that service is *always and necessarily* a form of manipulation. That is the logic of saying that the will to power is the fundamental dynamic of life; the ethic of service can only be a disguised form of the will to power. If that is true, then Christianity, which asserts that the fundamental dynamic of the universe is love, is ruled out as a dangerous and hypocritical delusion.

Nietzsche's logic leads him to celebrate raw power and to despise concern for the weak. When he does that it is difficult not to see him as one of the inspirations for Nazism and many of the other ills of the 20th century:

> What is good?—All that heightens the feeling of power, the will to power, power itself in man.
> What is bad?—All that proceeds from weakness.
> What is happiness?—The feeling that power *increases*—that a resistance is overcome.
> *Not* contentment, but more power; not peace at all, but war...
> The weak and ill-constituted shall perish: first principle of *our* philanthropy. And one shall help them to do so.
> What is more harmful than any vice?—Active sympathy for the ill-constituted and weak—Christianity...[10]

Here we begin to see something of the tragic irony of Nietzsche's philosophy. Having 'unmasked' the abuse of power in traditional values, morality and religion, he then proceeds to exalt the abuse of power. His philosophy becomes a kind of grotesque parody of Christianity. Instead of a Saviour come to rescue and restore humanity to its divine image and purpose, Nietzsche preaches that those who are willing can become Supermen, breaking free by their own will and power from the shackles of the past and leaving the rest to be swept away by the tide of history:

> *I teach you the Superman.* Man is something that should be overcome. What have you done to overcome him?
> All creatures hitherto have created something beyond themselves: and

---

9 *Thus Spoke Zarathustra*, pp 137f.
10 *Twilight of the Idols/The Antichrist*, pp 127f.

do you want to be the ebb of this great tide, and return to the animals rather than overcoming man?

What is the ape to men? A laughing-stock or a painful embarrassment. And just so shall man be to the Superman: a laughing-stock or a painful embarrassment...

The Superman is the meaning of the earth. Let your will say: The Superman *shall be* the meaning of the earth!

I entreat you, my brothers, *remain true to the earth*, and do not believe those who speak to you of superterrestrial hopes! They are poisoners, whether they know it or not.

They are despisers of life, atrophying and self-poisoned men, of whom the earth is weary: so let them be gone!

Once blasphemy against God was the greatest blasphemy, but God died, and thereupon these blasphemers died too. [11]

There could hardly be a more comprehensive rejection of the Christian doctrines of God, creation, salvation and the restoration of the created order to its divine purpose. On this view, meekness—a stance of willing submission before a loving creator—is a pernicious delusion.

To summarize: Nietzsche's view was that Christianity, religion, any form of idealism and in general 'the values and mythologies of the past had been... discredited.'[12] He scorned the attempts of Kant and others to rescue God, truth and morality. 'God was dead. But our new knowledge revealed not that we were impotent, but that we could become gods in his place. It would, Nietzsche thought, take us two centuries to face this transformation in all its aspects. But, once we had faced it, we would be free.'[13]

This was not going to come easily. He predicted that 'There will be wars such as there have never yet been on earth.'[14] The 20th century saw those wars, and much else besides. So Nietzsche leaves us with a choice. Are the horrors of 'the worst century there has ever been,'[15] merely the unfortunate by-products of the overthrow of Christianity and traditional moral values? Can we expect that in the future there lies some kind of Golden Age presided over by a race of Supermen? Or was Nietzsche wrong? Is it in fact the meek who will inherit the earth?

---

11 *Thus Spoke Zarathustra*, pp 41f.
12 Bryan Appleyard, *Understanding the Present—Science and the Soul of Modern Man* (Picador, 1992) pp 81f.
13 Appleyard, *ibid*.
14 Quoted in Appleyard, *ibid*.
15 Isaiah Berlin's verdict on the 20th century quoted in Michael Ignatieff, *Isaiah Berlin: A Life* (Chatto & Windus, 1998) p 301.

2
The Biblical Basis of Meekness

The Old Testament

The purpose of this booklet is to re-examine the teaching of Jesus on meekness and to restore it to the church for today as the true way to live. To do this we need to go back to its Old Testament roots. When Jesus announces 'Blessed are the meek for they shall inherit the earth' he is quoting from Psalm 37 (verse 11). The psalm is an extended meditation on the question of who will inherit the land. Will it be 'the wicked, who plot, scheme, default on debts, use raw power to gain advantage and seem thereby to flourish?'[16] The psalmist gives repeated assurance that, on the contrary, it will be those who trust in the Lord, commit their way to the Lord, are still before the Lord, wait for the Lord, hope in the Lord. The climax comes in verse 34:

> Wait for the Lord
>   and keep his way.
> He will exalt you to inherit the land;
>   when the wicked are cut off, you will see it.

'Wait' is the last in a series of imperatives and is repeated for emphasis. The waiting consists both in waiting for God to act—'waiting is necessary because God acts in his own time'[17]—and in waiting for God himself, for the joy of his presence.

A survey of Old Testament heroes shows how central is this waiting on God to their journey of faith. They exemplify the fact that the corollary of waiting for God is abstaining from taking matters into your own hands. Abram learns the blessing of this when he defers to Lot in allowing him the first choice of land in Genesis 13. Lot makes what proves to be the ill-fated choice of the plain of the Jordan, leaving Abram with the land of Canaan. God expresses his pleasure in Abram's refusal to go the way of the world by taking what seems the best: 'Lift up your eyes from where you are and look north and south, east and west. All the land that you see I will give to you and your offspring forever' (Genesis 13.14). Later on, when Abram does take matters into his own hands, the result is Ishmael, the child of his own efforts, not the child of promise. But Abram learns to wait, and so becomes Abraham, the father of Isaac and the 'father of many,' indeed of all who believe.

The story of Joseph is the story of a man humbled and shaped by his own

---

16 *NIV Study Bible* notes *ad loc.*
17 Alexander Ryrie, *Silent Waiting: The Biblical Roots of Contemplative Spirituality* (Canterbury Press, 1999) p 58.

experience of waiting for God to act through long years of humiliation, deprivation and disappointment. The result is a triumphant exaltation to a position of power and privilege.

Moses takes the law into his own hands by murdering an Egyptian he sees ill-treating an Israelite and as a result has to escape to the desert. There he spends many years waiting for God until he is called to a position of trust and power in which he will in a unique way 'take the law into his own hands' at Sinai and become known as the meekest man in all the earth (Numbers 12.3).

Samson is a man of immense spiritual power who consistently acts on impulse, taking matters into his own hands at every opportunity, frequently wreaking havoc and ending in shameful unfaithfulness to God. In prison, he too has to learn to wait. Having learnt, he ends his days with his last and greatest triumph for God by pulling down the temple of Dagon.

Saul, despite being anointed king of Israel, forfeits the favour of God by failing to wait for Samuel to offer sacrifice before Israel goes into battle with the Philistines. Instead he takes matters into his own hands and does it himself. David, by contrast, has to wait for many years after his anointing as king before he is able to assume the throne. During that time he more than once declines to take the law into his own hands by taking advantage of Saul's vulnerability in order to attack and destroy him. As a result he comes in time to rule over a great empire. He is the man after God's own heart, the man who looks to God for his vindication, who waits for God to act.

All these achieved much in this world by any standard. They did it by learning and practising meekness. Their meekness gave them power. This is not to say that meekness is a means to power, a canny way of getting God on your side. It is much more about God getting us on his side, so that we are fit and ready, in his time, to be caught up in his purposes. 1 Peter 5.6 expresses it well: 'Humble yourselves, therefore, under God's mighty hand, that he may lift you up in due time.'

A Russian Baptist testimony

Much hangs on the words 'due time'—due time is God's time, the time of his choosing. An illustration may help.

Herod's Dungeon[18] is the autobiography, thinly disguised as fiction, of a Russian Baptist named Yuri Grachev who spent the middle decades of the 20th century, from 1929 till the 1950s, in and out of Soviet penal institutions because of his faith. For much of that time he was without a Bible, so he came to adopt the practice of choosing every morning a verse from memory and meditating on that verse as the day proceeded. He referred to it as his 'golden verse.' One day his chosen verse was 'Blessed are the meek, for they shall inherit the earth.' He had just been released from the camps and was looking forward to being reunited with his family, but he still needed permission from

---

18   Yu S Grachev, *V Irodovoy Bezdne* (Moscow, 1994).

the local police in Ufa to return to his home region of Kuybyshev.

The queue at the police station was long and it moved slowly. Finally arriving at the desk he handed in his form, only to be told (what the Russian bureaucrat delights to tell the hapless man in any queue): 'It's not good enough. Go away and do it again with details of the places where you served your last sentence.' The police station was crowded: there was no room to write the whole thing out again with the necessary additions so he made for the post office. The job completed, Grachev returned to the police station and made to move straight to the officer in charge. But those in the queue objected: 'Get back to the end of the line!' As he was about to protest a still small voice reminded him of his text for the day: 'Blessed are the meek…' so he shut his mouth and went to the back of the queue.

Time passed and he saw the officer in charge disappear with a pile of documents and his secretary take over. Eventually he made it to the front of the queue again and handed in his papers.

'Why did you take so long?' said the secretary. 'The boss has taken all the papers away to sign. Why did you take so long to rewrite your request? You could have had it all sorted out and been on your way home to Kuybyshev today.'

Grachev explained about the queue. 'You should have been bolder,' she said. 'Tomorrow's a day off, so you'll have to come back the day after.'

Grachev went out and found a bench in the park, a voice whispering in his ear: 'So much for meekness! You won't get anywhere in this world like that—what you need is to be pushy, tough, rude.' But as he prayed he remembered having been told that, although there was no Christian community in Ufa, there were a few scattered believers, including a man working in a factory somewhere the other side of the Volga. Knowing no more than that he set off in search of this man and soon found himself at the gates of a factory asking if anybody knew of a believer who worked there. As he spoke he was directed to a man just emerging from the factory building, whom he thereupon greeted and found indeed to be a fellow Christian. The man invited him home, gave him food and shelter, introduced him to the small group of believers and asked him to stay for the opening of the new house of prayer which the authorities had recently granted them. Grachev stayed for a couple of days, giving and receiving spiritual encouragement and admonition. And when he returned to the police station his papers were processed and he was on the train home without a hitch.

Albeit in a small way, Grachev had found that providence is on the side of the patient soul who is prepared to set aside his own plans in favour of the will and way of God.

3
The Meekness of Christ

Christ describes himself as 'meek and lowly in heart' (Matthew 11.29). Apart from the Authorized Version, most English translations render the Greek *praüs* as 'gentle' instead of 'meek.' In so doing they break the verbal link with the beatitude 'Blessed are the meek, for they shall inherit the earth' (Matthew 5.5) and thus fail to convey the distinctive content of the word as defined by Psalm 37 and the wider Old Testament witness. They perhaps also miss Matthew's point that while the meekness of Moses was unique in his day, Jesus, as the new Moses, exemplifies a meekness unique in any day.

'Meek' occurs three times in Matthew, the third occasion being his account of the triumphal entry into Jerusalem in which he quotes Zechariah 9.9:

Tell the daughter of Zion:
Behold, your king comes to you,
meek and seated on an ass
and a colt the foal of an ass.

Here meekness is linked with kingship in a way that gives the lie to the idea that meekness is about feebleness or passivity. In a 'clearly messianic'[19] act Jesus enters Jerusalem in such a way as to encourage the crowds to believe that he is the true king. Of course the implicit message is that he is a particular kind of king—meekly mounted on a peaceable donkey rather than a warlike white charger—but a king all the same. He takes charge of the situation and uses it for his own ends. Or rather, he takes charge of the situation in such a way as to fulfil the Scriptures and to reveal the purpose of God. But there is no doubt that he is in charge.

The same is true of his life as a whole. Here is a man who does not allow himself to be pushed around. Even when he is under arrest, on trial and being nailed to a cross, the gospels convey a strong sense that he alone of all the actors in the drama is in control—the rest are puppets responding to forces manifestly outside their control. This is the paradox of meekness. Because at its heart is a complete submission to and delight in the will of God, there is also at its heart an unconquerable strength. The truly meek person is less likely than anybody to be a doormat. The meek draw strength from God for action and become capable of exploits and adventures which would elude the merely natural power of a forceful personality—but always and only within the will of God. As Jesus said, the Son can do nothing of his own accord, but only what he sees the Father doing (John 5.19).

---

19 N T Wright, *Jesus and the Victory of God* (SPCK, 1996) p 491.

Matthew's three references to meekness—the beatitude, the self-description of Jesus, and the Zechariah prophecy—together suggest an intriguing challenge to our culture's implicit belief that the good life is not a life lived in submission to God. In the figure of Christ we are faced with a man whose character and actions overflow with independence, originality, spontaneity, power, compassion and sheer vitality (all of which we would love to have but mostly lack). Yet these qualities are presented as the outcome of his relationship with and submission to God. You cannot have the one without the other. His life is the visible expression of the life of God fully realized in a human being.

Meekness and the Godhead

Here we come to another paradox. We may perhaps admit that meekness is all very well for a human being—submission to God is appropriate to our creaturely status. But if Jesus is not only fully human but also fully divine, where does such dependence fit into his experience? How can *God* submit to God?

The question is forced on us by the immediate context in Matthew 11 of the saying about meekness, beginning at verse 27:

> All things have been committed to me by my Father. No-one knows the Son except the Father, and no-one knows the Father except the Son and those to whom the Son chooses to reveal him.

Nowhere else in the Synoptics—excepting the Lukan parallel to this passage—does Jesus speak of himself in such exalted terms, even echoing the language of the fourth gospel with its repeated use of 'the Son' in absolute terms as a self-description. Jesus ascribes to himself a unique relationship with God in which the reciprocal nature of their mutual knowledge implies equality with God. Furthermore, he has the right to choose to whom he shall reveal this God. There could hardly be a more striking contrast with the claim to be meek and lowly. Self-exaltation and self-abasement appear to coexist side by side:

> Meekness and majesty,
> Manhood and deity,
> In perfect harmony,
> The man who is God...[20]

Is the harmony actually perfect, or are we dealing with an impossible union of incompatibles—a discord? In the history of the Christian church there have always been those who have tended to divide the divinity and the humanity of Christ from each other. I recently heard a speaker dealing with the gospel

---

[20] Graham Kendrick.

miracles refer to Jesus 'moving in the power of the Spirit rather than in his innate power and glory as God the Son.' The implication was clear: as a human being Jesus is dependent on the power of the Spirit, but such dependence does not apply to his divine nature.

The logic of this approach would be to say that the meekness of Christ—meekness is precisely about dependence—is a statement about his humanity but not his divinity. So, to return to Matthew 11 and putting things rather crudely, we would have to say that in verse 27 ('All things have been committed to me by my Father...') Christ is speaking out of his divinity, while in the following verses ('Come to me... for I am meek and lowly...') he is speaking out of his humanity. This seems hard to square with our intuitive sense that in Christ we meet an integrated personality rather than a Clarke Kent figure who sometimes disappears to change into Superman. Can we avoid this by finding a place for meekness within the Godhead? Is it possible that meekness is part not only of true humanity but also of the being of God himself?

The fourth gospel develops both facets of the person of Christ, his exalted position as the divine Son and his meek dependence on God, and it does this in such a way as to preclude the kind of separation of divine and human natures often suggested. John makes it explicit that it is 'the Son' who can do nothing of his own accord but only what he sees the Father doing (John 5.19). The Johannine Christ repeatedly states that he neither speaks nor acts from his own initiative but always in dependence upon the Father, reflecting all and only what the Father gives him.

Of course it could be said that this condition of dependence is only the result of the incarnation. In heaven the Son would regain what he always possessed in the first place—the right and capacity to take initiatives on his own account. But what right have we to say that dependence cannot be part of the life of the Godhead? This is an Islamic, not a Christian, doctrine: 'To be a son is less than divine, and to be divine is to be no one's son.'[21] A Trinitarian doctrine of God, which holds that the one God is three persons, can encompass dependence and interdependence between the persons.

The Self-emptying of Christ

The incarnate Christ obviously experienced limitation. He was not omnipresent. He was not omniscient. He specifically denied knowledge of the time of his return and often asked what look like genuine questions—how long has this child been sick? what do people say about me? and so on. Theologians have interpreted these limitations in a variety of ways. Some have suggested that when Paul spoke of the self-emptying (*kenosis*) of Christ in Philippians 2 he meant that the divine Son emptied himself of his divine attributes, laying aside omniscience, omnipresence and omnipotence. Others have spoken more cautiously of the self-reduction or self-retraction of God in

---

21 Quoted in Peter France, *Journey: A Spiritual Odyssey* (Chatto & Windus, 1998) p 63.

the incarnation. P T Forsyth makes the subtle observation that an infinite being who is incapable of reducing himself to the limits of the finite is to that extent finite and limited rather than infinite:

> If the infinite lies beyond the finite and outside it then the infinite is reduced to be but a larger finite; the infinite can only remain so if it have the power of the finite as well… The omniscience (or the omnipotence) of God does not mean that it is incapable of limitation but rather that with more power than finitude has it is also more capable of limitation. Only it is self-limitation; he limits himself in the freedom of holiness for the purposes of his own end of infinite love.[22]

For Forsyth and for many theologians, probably the majority, entry into time and into the necessary limitations of humanity made a radical difference to the capacities of the Son. And it may seem obvious that this is so. But it is not the picture the gospels present. They show Jesus experiencing tiredness and sleep and hunger and anger and even fear, but these never diminish his total responsiveness to the Father's will. Here is the heart and centre of his life: the relationship of Son to Father. It is a relationship of dependence, the relation of the lesser to the greater. 'The Father is greater than I' (John 14.28), just as a parent is in an important sense greater than his/her child. It is also true that 'I and the Father are one' (John 10.30), just as parent and child are one, sharing the same nature. And surely he is saying that these things are eternally true rather than merely conditions of the incarnation. He was the Father's Son in heaven before the incarnation and he is equally the Father's Son on earth. The relationship is the same and the dependence is the same.

The incarnation was not merely an assignment, a job to be done; it was the overflow of a relationship which is from all eternity, a relationship in which the Father speaks and the Son responds, because that is the nature of the Father-Son relationship. This is the implication of the credal statement that Christ is eternally begotten of the Father—there is an eternal dependence of the Son upon the Father. Why should this not encompass his knowledge and his power and every other aspect of his being and his life?

The self-emptying of which Paul speaks is best understood as the temporary shedding of the glory of heaven, a glory which is briefly revealed at the transfiguration, and the temporary acceptance of the weakness of the flesh, the taking into himself of tiredness, hunger and all the other limitations of human life. But there has been no change in the relationship of Son to Father.

---

[22] *The Person and Place of Jesus Christ* (London: Independent Press, 1909) pp 309, 311.

Obedience and fullness

Tom Smail asks:

> Can we talk of a divine obedience? Is there in God an ability not just to be first and command, but also to be second and obey? Is there within the one life of God a real subordination of the divine Son to the divine Father?'[23]

In answer he quotes Karl Barth:

> If God is in Christ, if what the man Jesus does is God's own work, this aspect of the self-emptying and self-humiliation of Jesus Christ as an act of obedience cannot be alien to God. But in this case we have to see here the other and inner side of the mystery of the divine nature of Christ and therefore of the nature of the one true God, that he himself is able and free to render obedience.[24]

This picture of the life of Christ as a life lived in dependence upon the Father is uncongenial to our culture's preoccupation with spontaneity and originality. We have been told that 'the very posture of receptivity means slavery.'[25] C S Lewis suggests how far we are from the spirit of the New Testament:

> 'Originality' in the New Testament is quite plainly the prerogative of God alone; even within the triune being of God it seems to be confined to the Father. The duty and happiness of every other being is placed in being derivative, in reflecting like a mirror.[26]

One of the difficulties that as children of the Enlightenment we have with this conception of meekness within the being of God is that it clashes with our commitment to equality. Lesslie Newbigin summarizes the Enlightenment view:

> The Enlightenment saw the human person as an autonomous centre of knowing and judging in such wise that any sort of heteronomy [any external, imposed authority] was to be rejected. The implication of this view is that each person has the right to develop his or her own potential to the maximum, limited only by the parallel rights of other persons. The governing principle, therefore, will be that of equality, since every person has equal rights. Equality will mean that—ideally—each one will have all that is needed for personal development, and each one will be the judge of what those needs are. Dependence of one upon another is—in this view—incompatible with human dignity.[27]

---

[23] *The Forgotten Father* (Hodder & Stoughton, 1980) pp 105f.
[24] *ibid* p 109.
[25] Karl Stern, *The Flight from Woman* (George Allen & Unwin, 1966) p 13.
[26] 'Christianity and Literature' in *Christian Reflections* (Collins, 1983) p 21.
[27] *The Other Side of 1984* (Geneva: World Council of Churches, 1984) p 56.

How much more then, we might add, is dependence of one person of the Godhead upon another incompatible with the dignity of deity. Newbigin goes on to outline the biblical view:
> The biblical vision of the human person is different at every point. In this vision there is no true humanity without relatedness, which means that mutual dependence is intrinsic to true humanity. The governing principle, therefore, is not equality but mutuality…[28]

Equality in the Enlightenment sense is not a biblical ideal. As an abstract noun it occurs only a handful of times in the entire biblical canon, notably in Philippians 2 where Christ is said to have rejected equality with God as 'something to be grasped,' and in 2 Corinthians 4 where Paul, in urging financial support between the churches, is commending exactly the mutuality described by Newbigin:
> Our desire is not that others might be relieved while you are hard pressed, but that there might be equality. At the present time your plenty will supply what they need, so that in turn their plenty will supply what you need.
> (2 Corinthians 8.13f)

The meekness of Christ holds out to us a vision of the perfectly fulfilled life as lived in submission to God. In Christ meekness is revealed as intrinsic to deity as well as to humanity. To submit to God is not, as the Enlightenment implied, to opt for oppression but to find liberation. The meekness of Christ rebukes human pride and pretensions to independence as foolish and misguided. Limitation is intrinsic not only to humanity but to deity as well. Absolute freedom—the rejection of all limits—is the denial of relationship. To be in relationship with another is to accept limits on your freedom. The obvious example is marriage, in which two people vow to limit their freedom by committing themselves to one another unconditionally—sickness, poverty, indeed any change of fortune are now ruled out as reasons for changing your mind about this person.

Personal relationships, deriving ultimately from the Trinity itself, are a fundamental part of reality. And therefore limits are fundamental too. This goes back to Eden. The limitation on independent knowledge set by God in the garden was not an arbitrary imposition on the human race to spoil our fun or a trap set to trip us up. It was a reflection of the fact that dependence is the way to fullness of life and to refuse that dependence is to choose death. Christ in his meekness models for us what it means to live out of dependence on God and so find the abundant life he promised. There is no other way. All things come from God and we can only receive them if we are willing to receive them from him.

---

[28] *ibid* p 56.

4
The Power of Meekness

Meekness is the willingness to let God be God. We give back to God what Adam and Eve stole in Eden, and in return receive from God what they lost—the capacity, under God, to rule. We begin to experience the kingdom of God in which, because his rule is again acknowledged, we regain our capacity to 'reign in life' (Romans 5.17). Meekness is about regaining the loss of control involved in the Fall. Humanity is constantly striving to control God, circumstances and other people. In the long run it is a losing battle. When Paul lists the fruit of the Spirit in Galatians 5 meekness comes next to self-control. It is ourselves that we need to learn to control, not God or other people.

Prayer

Meekness is at the heart of Christian spirituality. Pagan spirituality is about trying to control God by whatever means can be found. It is humanity's desperate attempt to master God and, through God, the circumstances of life. In Christian prayer, by contrast, the roles are reversed: 'the main object is to be mastered.'[29] This can come as something of a shock. I remember the day in church when, as we said the Lord's Prayer before receiving communion, I suddenly realized that my attention did not properly engage until we arrived at the petition 'Give us today our daily bread.' All the bits about God's name, God's kingdom and God's will passed me by as of no personal concern. What I was interested in were the petitions that touched me. This is a radical, and disabling, misunderstanding of the nature of prayer.

The Lord's Prayer turns the natural human conception of prayer on its head. Praying this prayer is a kind of death to self. It requires us to put the hallowing of God's name and the coming of his kingdom before our own concerns. We have to give up the attempt to control God with our demands.

So what then is the point of prayer? If it is not the means by which we get what we want, what is it? The answer must be that it is God's way, or one of them, by which he gets us involved in his purposes. Praying for the coming of God's kingdom is one of the ways in which we become co-workers with God. This is part of the point of the image of the yoke used by Jesus. As we take his yoke upon us, by prayer and by work, we align ourselves with him and his purposes and are empowered to see things happen beyond anything that our own capacities would allow. Hence the astonishing promises of Christ about the power of prayer—moving mountains, anything you ask, and so on. Understood as *carte blanche* to do what we like these are absurd and those who approach them in this spirit are destined for disappointment. But understood

---

[29] Richard Foster, *Prayer: Finding the Heart's True Home* (Hodder & Stoughton, 1992) p xi.

as one aspect of the promise to the meek that they shall inherit the earth, they make perfect sense. Why should not God give authority to his trusted and trustworthy co-workers, submitted as they are to his will, to ask for and receive whatever is necessary for the work of the kingdom in their sphere?

Elijah's contest with the prophets of Baal is a case in point. The prophets spend a whole day in increasingly frenzied attempts to get Baal to respond to their call for fire to come down on the sacrifice. When mere petition fails they resort to self-mutilation. But this too produces no result. Praying, prophesying and slashing themselves with spears and swords achieve nothing. The writer sadly sums up the futility of pagan worship: 'But there was no response, no one answered, no one paid attention' (1 Kings 18.29).

Elijah, by contrast, prays a simple prayer:

> O LORD, God of Abraham, Isaac and Israel, let it be known today that you are God in Israel and that I am your servant and have done all these things at your command.
>
> (1 Kings 18.36)

Elijah is not getting his own way but working with God to see God's will done. He is responding to the leading of God, doing, as Christ did, all and only that which he saw the Father doing (John 5.19). And lest it be thought that the spirit of Elijah's actions is in some way exceptional in the kingdom of God, the New Testament makes it clear that he was 'a human being like us' (James 5.17). Ordinary people can see God do amazing things as they pray. The one condition placed on this effectiveness in prayer is that it be 'the prayer of the righteous' (James 5.16). Righteousness is essentially right relationship. If we are rightly related to God in meekness and submission, then we can pray as Elijah prayed. We may not see fire come from heaven, but we will surely experience prayer that is 'powerful and effective.'

Some may object that this is a misguided view of God, of prayer and of the place and responsibility of humanity on this earth. Paul Oestreicher writes:

> Within creation there is autonomy and within that autonomy there is given to us, who are made in God's image, a real measure of freedom. That is the limited extent of our power. Yes, we have power. We may not like it. We may prefer to ascribe power to God. But it is ours. We are, within the complex limitations of this created order, plenipotentiaries…
>
> In consequence, the kind of prayer that tells God what to do is a rejection of our true role, a refusal to accept responsibility. It is not God who starts or ends wars. We do. God does not feed hungry children or let them starve. We do. God does not rule or overrule. The world is not his puppet theatre.[30]

---

[30] Paul Oestreicher, *The Double Cross* (DLT, 1986) p 97.

Of course Oestreicher is right about war and hungry children. Prayer is not a means by which we can evade our responsibilities or a substitute for action. What he misses is that the freedom and the power God has given us include the freedom to submit to him and the power of the prayer for the coming of his kingdom. To cooperate with God in prayer is to see our freedom and power fulfilled rather than negated or abrogated. In this way God's rule becomes real 'on earth as in heaven.'

Spiritual Warfare

The power of meekness is also shown in the way we respond to being attacked. The natural human response is to fight back, giving as good as we get. Meekness requires that instead we wait for God's response. 1 Peter describes Christ's response to suffering: 'When they hurled their insults at him, he did not retaliate; when he suffered, he made no threats. Instead, he entrusted himself to him who judges justly' (1 Peter 2.23). Christians who suffer unjustly are urged to do the same: 'commit themselves to their faithful Creator' (1 Peter 4.19). The ultimate rationale for this stance is found in the New Testament teaching about spiritual warfare. Paul insists that 'our struggle is not against flesh and blood, but against the rulers, against the authorities, against the powers of this dark world and against the spiritual forces of evil in the heavenly realms' (Ephesians 6.12). When our discipleship leads us into realms of conflict we need to recognize the reality behind the appearance. We may experience human attacks of various kinds, but it is not the people involved who are our real enemies. They are caught up in a spiritual battle of which they may be unaware. In this situation meekness is expressed in gentleness towards those who would harm us. We do not have to hit back because the ultimate issue is with God, who has already in Christ defeated the powers of darkness. But neither are we meant to be doormats, for God calls us to 'stand firm' (Ephesians 6.14).

We need to be very clear that meekness is not a craven capitulation in the face of evil and injustice. The armour of God is given us, not so that we can sit around and do nothing, but 'so that when the day of evil comes, you may be able to stand your ground, and after you have done everything, to stand' (Ephesians 6.13). Having 'done everything' may include speaking the truth to those who are lying, challenging injustice and taking risks with our own safety. The meekness of Christ is seen both in his fearsome denunciations of his opponents (because he is simply saying what the Father has given him to say) and in his silence before his accusers at his trial (because that is what the Father gives him at that moment). He is never a doormat because in every situation he looks not to the human agents involved but to the will and word of God for that moment.

Control

If meekness is the willingness to let God be God, it is equally the willingness to let other people be themselves. The gentleness which is one aspect of meekness is a strong kind of gentleness which holds us back from inappropriate interference in other people's lives. It is a respect for the image of God in another human being which cautions us to tread warily in their presence. Because it is the recognition that God is in control, meekness empowers us in two directions: firstly, not to be controlled by others; and secondly, not to attempt to impose control upon them. Jesus exemplifies both. He is never controlled by those around him. He resists every demand that does not fit the Father's will. In fact he impresses the reader of the gospels as the only truly free person on the scene, even (or perhaps supremely) in the events of the Passion. Being free, Jesus also respects the freedom of others. The classic example is the rich young ruler's rejection of Jesus' invitation to sell all his possessions for the benefit of the poor and follow him. Jesus makes no attempt to change the man's mind, not out of indifference, for he 'looked at him and loved him' (Mark 10.21), but because he will not violate the dignity and responsibility of human choice.

Codependency

I propose to focus the discussion of control in an examination of the behaviour pattern known as codependency. Codependency is a form of addiction, specifically a 'people addiction,' which is often associated with people caught up in relationship with those who are addicted either to processes (such as gambling or computer games) or to substances (such as alcohol, food or drugs). In an increasingly addiction-prone society it is important to understand the spiritual roots of the problem. (That addiction is, amongst other things, a spiritual problem has long been recognized by, for instance, Alcoholics Anonymous, who insist that trust in a Higher Power is essential to recovery.) Codependency has been defined as:

> A self-focused way of life in which a person blind to his or her true self continually reacts to others, being controlled by and seeking to control their behaviour, attitudes, and/or opinions, resulting in spiritual sterility, loss of authenticity, and absence of intimacy.[31]

The term codependency arose in the context of treatment given to the families of substance-abusers such as alcoholics. It became clear that the problem in alcoholic families is often not only the substance-abuse by one member of the family. There is often also the diseased behaviour of other family members, typically the spouse, who allows him or herself to be controlled by the alcoholic's behaviour. The codependent also makes futile attempts to control that

---

[31] Nancy Groom, *From Bondage to Bonding* (NavPress, 1991) p 21.

behaviour, thus depriving the substance-abuser of the dignity of responsibility for their own actions.

Codependency is not confined to the families of substance-abusers. Many people manifest it to some extent. The question is how far it damages our relationships, both with God and with other people. Codependents

> live at the mercy of others' demands or expectations, and… end up feeling *used* and *powerless*. We look to others for permission to do something or be someone, and the loss of empowerment results in a profound anger or depression we can neither change nor understand. Without choice, codependents feel driven, helpless, victimized.[32]

Wherever we see people out of control, experiencing loss of choice and even the loss of the sense of self, we are probably encountering some degree of codependency. Codependency ranges from the tragic (the woman whose life is focused on concealing her husband's drinking from outsiders) to the laughable (the person who turns to a friend in a shop and says 'Do I like this shirt?'). The codependent finds it very hard to let God be God, to live out of a relationship of trust and submission before him which frees and empowers for healthy living. To allow God to be in control is too frightening, and so the codependent resorts to strategies for taking matters into his or her own hands. It is a form of rebellion against God, though it may mask itself as pious and committed to good works. It is a condition to which Christians are far from immune, because 'codependent behaviours often masquerade as Christian virtues… Losing one's self and sacrificing for others seem to be the biblical epitome of piety.'[33] The codependent typically wants to look good and is therefore committed to a lifelong project of 'impression management.' Controlling behaviour can easily be mistaken by the superficial observer for self-sacrificial love.

An Example of Codependency

The story told by Hilary and Piers du Pré of their relationship with their sister Jackie is a good illustration of codependency in action.[34] Jacqueline du Pré was one of the most brilliant cellists of her generation, but she was, according to Hilary in an interview with *The Times*,[35] a tortured soul who 'unwittingly destroyed' those closest to her. The family never said 'No' to her. The most extreme manifestation of this came when 'for 16 months between 1971 and 1972, [Hilary] allowed Jackie (who was still married to Daniel Barenboim) to have an affair with Kiffer, her husband of ten years, and move in with them at their home.'[36] *The Times'* interviewer probes Hilary's motiva-

---

32 *ibid* p 25 (italics original).
33 *ibid* pp 28f.
34 Hilary and Piers du Pré, *A Genius in the Family* (Chatto & Windus, 1997).
35 4 October 1997
36 *ibid*.

tion and is told that 'not to have done so would have precipitated her sister into total breakdown.' The interviewer responds that this is 'an extraordinary act of love.' Hilary denies this:

> I wouldn't have done anything else. I couldn't have. I did it because that was what had to happen. It was the only way I could cope with the situation and with myself at the time. It was all I could do, and in the end it still wasn't enough.

'Not enough?' the interviewer responds in astonishment. 'No,' says Hilary. 'Because she got multiple sclerosis and she died.' There speaks the codependent, controlled by the needs of another person and taking responsibility for that person's life to the point almost of absurdity—as if Hilary was responsible for or could have prevented Jackie's MS.

The roots of this go deep. But one crucial moment in the development of Hilary's way of dealing with her sister came at a music festival in Purley when Hilary was eleven and Jackie eight. They both received medals, but before the presentation was made to Jackie a speech was given praising her extraordinary talent. Hilary was forgotten and ran off down a dark corridor to cry. When she came back she realized nobody had missed her. Then she made a decision:

> At the Purley festival, I realized that the only way to protect myself was to go and support Jackie, and there's nothing wonderful about that at all… I was purely looking after myself. Can you understand that? Have I made that clear?[37]

Hilary is very insistent that this incident, the lifestyle that grew out of it, and her consent to her husband's affair with Jackie were not acts of love, of free self-giving for the good of another, but ways of controlling the situation so that she could survive. The focus was all the time on self, whatever the outward appearance may have suggested to the contrary. This is a classic instance of Luther's description of sinful humanity as *'incurvatus in se'*—turned in upon the self. The codependent exemplifies the sinner's refusal of a meek dependence on God and the empowerment that flows from it, and the consequent decision to find ways of taking matters (including other people) into one's own hands—and ways of coming out looking good into the bargain.[38] The only cure is to let God be God in one's life and in the increasing security of that begin to allow other people to be themselves.

---

[37] ibid.
[38] None of this is intended as a criticism of or judgment on Hilary du Pré, who demonstrates both self-awareness and honesty. But her story, already in the public domain, offers a clear illustration of the issues involved.

5
Growing in Meekness

Where does the power of meekness come from? By what mechanism does it become part of us? Meekness is not a natural characteristic of fallen humanity. It must not be confused with the compliance of the weak person. The weak have as much to learn about meekness as the strong. In this we are all in the same boat. Paul says that meekness is the fruit of the life and work of the Spirit in us. Sometimes this is interpreted to mean that we have nothing to do with the process, that it will happen willy-nilly. But this is a misunderstanding of Paul; Galatians 5 on the fruit of the Spirit is followed by Galatians 6:

> Do not be deceived; God is not mocked, for you reap whatever you sow. If you sow to your own flesh, you will reap corruption from the flesh; but if you sow to the Spirit, you will reap eternal life from the Spirit
> (Galatians 6.7f).

Grace invites a response—we are being asked to cooperate with God. The action of God in our lives can be represented in terms of a triangle:[39]

```
           The Action of the Holy Spirit
                      △
Ordinary events of life        Spiritual disciplines
```

At the apex is the Holy Spirit, who directs our lives and energizes our disciplines. At the base of the triangle is our daily life, 'where we dwell with God and our neighbours.'[40] The 'ordinary events of life' which pertain particularly to the growth of meekness in us are the experiences of 'wilderness.' Abraham,

---

[39] Adapted from Dallas Willard, *The Divine Conspiracy: Rediscovering our Hidden Life in God* (Fount, 1998) p 380.
[40] *ibid* p 380.

Joseph, Moses and David all went through a wilderness experience of some kind, which involved prolonged periods of waiting for the fruition of God's promises in their lives. Meekness appears to be inseparable from the experience of having our self-reliance broken. As we learn the true limits of our own power to take matters into our own hands, so we are ready to cry out to God. We learn to 'wait for the Lord and keep his way.'

It is characteristic of the wilderness experience to feel that God has abandoned us. In fact this is a time when the Spirit is specially and continually at work in us, leading us both *into* the wilderness (Matthew 4.1, Mark 1.12) and *in* the wilderness (Luke 4.1). He takes us into the place where our own resources dry up, and works in us while we are there. While we are there the agenda is death to the demanding spirit that wants to 'take the waiting out of wanting' and the breaking of our self-reliance, which is the substance of the temptations that Christ is exposed to. Satan tempts Christ in a variety of ways—to do his own thing, to do Satan's thing, to force the hand of God. What he must choose instead is a meek dependence on God. He must affirm his willingness to keep in step with the Spirit. Only so can he defeat the enemy and fulfil his ministry.

For him the battle lasts only forty days, though no doubt it makes up in intensity for what it lacks in duration. For the heroes of the Old Testament it is a matter of years, sometimes very long years. Many Christians have had to wait a long time to see God fulfil his promises to them.

The Power of Meekness

We began with Nietzsche's passionate longing for all that is life-giving and life-enhancing. That, I suggest, rather than the Will to Power, is the real underlying dynamic at work in us. We long for life. Jesus came to give life, life in all its fullness. Our culture's obsession with experience, with sensation, with the mood and fashion of the moment, is a longing for life. The tragedy is that we look for it in the wrong places, mistakenly supposing that we can grab for ourselves what can only be received from God. The meekness of Jesus shows the right way—a radical openness and obedience to the life of God himself continuously offered to us.

Jesus makes two promises related to meekness. The first is that the meek will inherit the earth. They may not look impressive or powerful but they will receive and achieve more in the long run than those who go it alone without God. The second is that those who learn from the meekness of Christ will find rest for their souls. In contrast to the common experience that high achievement means high levels of stress, they make an impact without destroying themselves or those close to them. It is surely the perfect combination—the best of both worlds.